The

Joanne M. Clarkson —i

The Fates

Joanne M.Clarkson

Joanne M. Clarkson

May the beauty of words always bring good Fortune!

Bright Hill Press

Treadwell, New York 2017

The Fates

Joanne M. Clarkson

Bright Hill Press Poetry Award Series, No. 23
2016 Winner - Chosen by Richard Foerster

Cover Art and Book Design: Bertha Rogers
Editor in Chief: Bertha Rogers
Assistant to the Editor: Lawrence E. Shaw
Author Photograph: Jim Clarkson

Library of Congress Cataloging-in-Publication Data

Names: Clarkson, Joanne M., author.
Title: The fates / by Joanne M. Clarkson.
Description: First edition. | Treadwell : Bright Hill Press, 2017. | Series:
   Bright Hill Press poetry award series ; no. 23 | Includes bibliographical
   references and index.
Identifiers: LCCN 2017022843 | ISBN 9781892471857 (alk. paper)
Classification: LCC PS3603.L3826 A6 2017 | DDC 811/.6--dc23
LC record available at https://lccn.loc.gov/2017022843

The Fates is published by Bright Hill Press. Bright Hill Press, Inc., a non-for-profit, 501(c)
(3) literary and educational organization that was founded in 1992. The organization is
registered with the New York State Department of State, Office of Charities Registration.
Publication of *The Fates* is made possible, in part, with public funds from the Literature
Program of the New York State Council on the Arts and with the support of Governor
Andrew Cuomo and the New York State Legislature.

Editorial Address:
Bright Hill Press, Inc., 94 Church Street
Treadwell, NY 13846-4607
Voice: 607-829-5055; Fax: 607-829-5054
Website: www.brighthillpress.org - E-mail: wordthur@stny.rr.com

Acknowledgements

Grateful acknowledgment is made
to the following print and online publications
for poems that originally appeared or are forthcoming in them:

Alaska Quarterly Review: "Hired Horses at Seaside"
Amoskeag: "The Cursive 'I'"
Arcana: The Tarot Poetry Anthology: "The Nine of Cups"
Ascent: "The New CPR"
The Baltimore Review: "The Stone Masons" (First prize winner)
Bloodroot: "Hotel ZZZ"
The Chattahoochee Review: "Judy Macaroski"
Crab Creek Review: "Planet of the Hired Men"
Edge: "Bloodstone"
Emrys: "Survivor:" (Nancy Dew Taylor Award)
Fjords Review: "Slaughterhouse Wife"
The Great American Poetry Show: "Fire Mare"
The Healing Muse: "The Breath Mirror"
Literary Mama: "Swedish Spoon"
The Midwest Quarterly: "Eyes Like Trunk or Wingtip"
Minerva Rising: "Icarus' Sister"
Modern Poetry Quarterly Review:
"Atropos the Fate Dismantles Her Own Altar"
Naugatuck River Review: "Wound and Stone"
Nimrod International Journal: "Mother of Phobia"
Not Somewhere Else But Here,
*Sundress Publications: A Contemporary Anthology
of Women and Place:* "In the Millinery Shop"
Perfume River Review: "Ouija After Midnight,"
"The Goodbye Skin," and "Grief Code"
Pinyon: "The Weatherman's Widow"
Poem Your Heart Out Anthology: "Last Straw"
Pontoon: "Lost Twin" and "The Nine of Cups" (reprinted)
Pooled Ink: "Klotho the Fibre Goddess Describes Fate"
(Northern Colorado Writers first prize winner)
Pudding Magazine: "Auditioning Sisters" and "Thoroughbred"
Pulse, Voices from the Heart of Medicine: "Teaching the Wound"
Rhino: "The Mannequin's Comb"
Saranac Review: "Birth of the North Wind" and "Old Growth"
Switched-on Gutenberg: "The Weather Letters"
Switchgrass Review: "All the Horses Are Dying" and

Joanne M. Clarkson —v

Acknowledgments (Continued)

"Thrift Store Cashmere"
Tampa Review Online: "News People"
Third Wednesdays: "Escalators"

Special thanks:

Artist Trust for a GAP grant to complete this manuscript
My mentors at the Colrain Manuscript Conference in Truchas, NM
Bryan Willis and members of the Pan Writers Group
My fellow board members of the Olympia Poetry Network

Contents

Part III

—For Esther and Veronika
women of will and courage, who left Sweden and Slovakia
in the nineteen-teens for a new Fate that, generations later, became my life.

—And for Jim, with love.

Part I

Klotho the Fibre Goddess Describes Fate

Anything can be spun: mare's tail, thistle,
    free will. My task is dust
and the sticky milk of love. My birthright:

a spindle, phallic tool, daemon of destiny.
    From nothing I pull anima. I am
the umbilical sister. Anything can be

spun: linen, ink, deception. Which
    is true: the silk worm or its silk?
I have honed my skill more than any

young seductress. Yet in temples I'm the
    spinster, Deity whose marble arms
long ago fell away, influence fading

with the first trip or tangle. Those who believe
    hang my image in genome labs
where anything can be spun: prodigies,

left-handedness and chance, the crucial
    knot. I work my treadle
and a hundred couples climb into

backseats, let out rope and ribbons
    with their fetal curl. With all its flaws
how I love this task. First to cradle

not the child, but its hunger, its wail,
    strands within its pliable skull: anything
        that can be spun.

The Mannequin's Comb

This morning I washed a dying woman's
hair. She sighed with caress,
remembering. Tonight

I bathe a baby whose scalp is still
birthing its brain, bone cupping trust
like an unfolding flower. Outside
sweet peas sing. My

grandmother worked in her sister's
millinery shop. Lace and feathers, straw
and felt. She shaped spring out of
satin and autumn's velvet from the tilt
of a brim, all women
mysterious. In the picture window each
weekday, she arrayed the
mannequin's pale oval, creating face
from the shadow
of a veil. Emotion with the teeth
of her comb. My hands

know so many small gestures. This
morning I washed
a woman to her bone, lying
when I said that hair
didn't come away, that it was only
thread and could be
mended.

Auditioning Sisters

Hazy heroine, I sense you
   beside me at the grocery
store choosing ripe cantaloupe
    and the freshest bunch of
      lettuce. I am

what might have been. You
   died before I was conceived, tiny curl
blue-cold in a crib.

I have resurrected a thousand versions
   of you, my older sister, with hair
dark like hers while mine was lighter, even
    at birth, like our father's mother.

I remember a woman who miscarried five
   times telling me she owned those souls
"for just a little while" as she wrapped
    pink blankets in her mind
around the whisper of a body.

How long do we have each other? Until we
   move away, forget a phone
number, reach some hidden quota of knowing?

I scan strangers in audiences, airports, carnivals
   and produce aisles, auditioning
sisters, hoping that death is myth, that you were
    kidnapped or left behind

and we recognize each other like dust
   rubbed off a mirror revealing one silver
self, character I always write
    in first person.

Watching for Morning

There's a tide to all this: seventeen
houseboats rock the harbor,
waking to gulls. I watch from
the bank above, nesting the way
I often do, in my mind's eye.

I see the shudder of a small red
door that sticks a little then swings.
A figure—she—I can tell
it's a woman under baggy plaid,
sweeps the deck, tidies, readying the day.

Then she stands, just stands, legs
slightly apart for balance, looking west not
east, arms slack. She

has lost someone. A man
most likely and with him her
womanhood. Children by a first love
who have given themselves away.

Out on open water, the first canvas lifts,
unfurls and is pregnant with wind.
Journey is brisk, bucking. I can
tell she longs for sail even more than
for a mate. I would send her one
if I could, then take her place
on the houseboat at dawn.

Thrift Store Cashmere

Volunteer sorting boxes of after
    life, I have kept faith and today
it arrived, an ivory-colored coat, soft
    as a soul, corresponding
      to my bones.

Second-hand, it is impossible to know whether
    boredom or misfortune brought it
here as I slip my arm through a
    sleeve and become the ease
of warm woolen breath.

I press button after rhinestone
    button through the perfect holes
noticing how she strengthened them
    with a different shade of
thread. A glamorous shroud.

Turning up the collar, I unfold a single
    hair as though she slipped her
      helix here to spy on afterlife

or sacrifice: her donation to the poor
    that she wore when her lover
left, or her soft scent that someone grieving
    could no longer bear
      to keep near.

Birth of the North Wind

I wrap the baby in my old coat and take her
out under cedar to hear winter
begin. Wind is high, from the north, north-
east. It has an open-mouthed sigh just short
of a howl. It lauds absent
blossoms. She lifts her face
to it, lips parted, offering her first
word, a yes to old, old
mountains that she remembers like hunger.
Her cheeks glow with the story of
firelight. Her tiny hands wriggle out of
wool to grasp the wind's invisible
hide full of teeth, sorrow and a
tameness only the very young
understand. Her perfect cloud of breath
trails away becoming sunset, becoming
snow, guiding the north wind
southward.

The Idiom for Shame

She quickly learned the idiom for
    shame, every syllable a misstep.
How they made her beg for food
    as though hunger and taste
        could make her fluent.

They had come to this country for
    work. Her mother had said, "You
are young. You can learn." But she
    never said it in English.

English. Rushing over her like cold water
    making her sputter and drown
confusing the way to air, her tongue
    swollen, lips pale as a corpse.

Immigrant. Ignorant.

And when the school room taunts had finally
    turned toward some other clumsy child
and she was left to the bliss of silence

even this was shattered by the loud
    transgression of her name: The huge
bellowing man standing in the impossible
    length of hallway
with her small sister who had wet her
    pants, unable to ask
        for a bathroom.

She took the hand of her younger shivering
    self and headed out into traffic
having no idea how to map the ocean
    toward the wrong word for home.

Icarus's Sister

She twists to examine her naked back
  in the polished metal mirror,
searches the itch under skin, buds arching
  under shoulder bones.

Gathering uncombed hair, she raises her arms,
  senses ascent. Next she faces
forward, hands flat, traces
  her chest for nubs opposite the ache

of wings, tests for balance that will signal
  the season when she can
soar, scapulas shimmering in the
  glimpse of first light.

She should be the child to fly,
  requiring no wax, nothing stolen
from geese or swan.
    It is time.

Suffering only the small
  bruises that come with the risk of self-love,
she lifts off, strokes into morning head-on,
    circles the willing world,

her ecstatic shadow caressing a herd of mountain goats,
  a school of herring, marshland of wild iris
and a farmer's son resting at noon,
  biting into his peasant bread.

She presses her legs together,
  points her toes. Hugs herself,
gathering in bare arms
  the reflection of her splendor.

Ouija after Midnight

Four just this side of thirteen, vowing
wakefulness, wishing futures
and gossamer of ghosts. They gather
around the moveable board. Try light fingers
on planchette. How gracefully it drifts

from letter to number, arcing between
yes and no. Their fear
is wonderful. They giggle and glance
at each other asking first
about this or that
boy, who likes who, and what about

the math quiz. But after midnight
the mood gutters likes a black candle. Shadows
add their hands and the world
widens. Questions

grow an afterlife of girls
gone missing. Forest of misstep. Man
with a sack of kittens. How they could save
only one. They know then

that the future is more than crushes. That something
stalks dark gardens, drags slender
wrists to the verge of a bottomless
pond where all reflections sleep, masked
in young faces. Winter is longer

than summer could ever be. And in the morning
when the board is just a game, they still
tip-toe and whisper, seeing in every corner
their own indelible ghosts.

Judy Macaroski

Forty years later I still know her name
that girl I glimpse in the overgrown
front yards of unkept houses,
shoulder-length weed-brown hair
blowing across a face
that does not notice me.
Bare-footed, she brazened my father's
building sites scavenging a bent nail,
a shaved wood curl.

During lunch breaks and smoke breaks
the workmen called to her
laughing at how she sassed back
hands on her almost hips,
how she stroked the hair out of her eyes
with the bitten moons of fingernails
leaving a tan smudge.

The wind is steep with rain. I drive
a mile out of my way to avoid that house,
the last one he built. I can taste
the gray meal as he described at the dinner table
the little girl who played in the weeds
how she wasn't me in my carefully braided
best, my tight unscuffed shoes,
my immaculate hands folded on my desk,
in my lap, daughter of obedience.

How my mother never let me near
the racket of saws and hammers
or the hum of the cement truck
as the neighborhood kids gathered around
for the foundation pour.

And when he died when I was ten
she was the last to see him
that girl with holes at the knee
without a coat even in November
the girl with the crooked nail in her fist
while mine was empty.

Grief Code

—for JBS

They rattle as I ease the lowest dressing
table drawer open. Lost seeds. How summer
sounds, dying. I bend down to examine
six medicine bottles dated
more than thirty years ago. Labels peeling,
the few pills desiccated, flaking
into impotent powder. Prescribed for a woman
I have never met with your familiar
surname. Neighbors told me
that there had been a daughter. Joan

whose profile dusts unadorned
walls. It's all grief code, the pauses, syllables
choked back. I had been searching
for your bandages, the ones for legs swollen now
and weeping. Wounds erupting again and
the next month, forced by a faulty
heart. I must have heard wrong; thought
you directed me to search in this vanity, where,
instead of gauze, I unmask
a small coffin full of all the remedies
you offered for her ransom. On days

of immortality, when health seems permanent
as silver-caned seas, when knees fold
easily, do you genuflect searching for
jewels, the ones you gave on birthdays
year after year all bleached
shell white? Or do you save this journey

for worst midnights planning, in your madness,
to eat what's left yourself, your penance
of poisons? Gently, I push the drawer
closed, hear feverish chatter, one
finger typing the small print of her name.

Slaughterhouse Wife

When he comes home, his clothes are soaked
with souls. I wash the bawling
from his sleeves. Spatter laughs
in shapes of faces: crooked ear, the long nose.

We never speak of it. He eats in front of
sports. Men colliding with huge shoulders. He yells
and yells with fists. He answers me
with yawns. Morning

I hand him the hump of his lunch pail. Wonder
if we will ever have children. His hands
are huge, beefy at the bases. His arms a permanent
swing. I know like a map, the back of his
neck, the hairline. I send him off clean.

All day alone I hear wind bellowing. There's a stink
in the leaves. I stop myself the small
unkindnesses. Untwist my face from glances
in the street. Nothing wrong with honest
work. The whole town feeds. I wash
vegetable legs, wincing as I trim them.

Often his porch-step is late, beer heavy. He
stares past me into warm rooms of some unknown
reckoning. I reach to take him in my
arms. He hands me the bleeding meat.

Mother of Phobia

I sweep porch steps this morning
brooming away what was spun last night
in girders and grids of dread. I dust
between railings.

Behind me you finish your milk, grab
your backpack. School bus idles
further up the block. You pause
at the first step, check my handiwork,
then run. Our ritual.

I search the invisible spaces
kaleidoscope of pristine fear
the barest touch the worst
tingle at necklines igniting
every suggestion of nerve.

What engendered this untaught whimper
that you may never outgrow?

I have considered making you face your harmless,
leggy enemy, much smaller than a penny, that I spy
now sheltered in the ell of a step

or how I might heal you, pointing out her
beautiful brown sister settled between fern
and late Peace rose in her own angled blossom.

For now, I settle for one simple act I can still
offer you: I sweep again, snagging the offending
spider and carry her, bristle bound,
out back near the maple where I free her
amid leaf fall and an end of seasons,
my own unnamable fear.

Swedish Spoon

—for Esther

Too small for soup, too valuable for every day,
I remember you polishing and polishing, turning
a rag black to spring silver from the mouth
of a tiny utensil imprinted Sweden. Treasure

stored in velvet, now mine. Was it
your gift or your mother's or her
mother's, passing hand to hand through
centuries of women, more fit for decoration
than hunger? Today while raiding

the silver chest, counting place settings
for the next family celebration, daughter
of my daughter, two, unearths this metal
just her size. She demands Cheerios.

I watch her eat the tiny rings one
by one, looking back into sweetness.
How you rationed sugar, scooped less
than a teaspoon, sifted it into tea,
tea-with-milk, silver tea you called it, my
grown-up drink at three or four

that you poured into chipped China
blowing across to cool. The cradle
of this spoon exactly fits my thumb.
When I rub and rub some part of you
reappears: the darkness, the shine.

Bloodstone

January birth, my grandmother gave me
    a garnet ring. I had never seen
that facet of blood. She wasn't wealthy, wore
      the same black gown every
holiday pinned with a different
      brooch. In summer

a satin shadow. I slipped her gift on my
    sinister hand, afraid I would outgrow
it, lose it like destiny. She loved to fold

my hands in her chilly ones, skin mobile
    as the fabrics she sewed, penance
of machines and needles for vain
      women's bodies. Other girls

were jealous of my ring that flashed
    when I spiked a volleyball or curried
the manes of imaginary mares. I wore

it to bed throughout my teens. Only when pregnant
    did I switch it to my little finger. When married
crossed it to my dexterous hand. I am older
    then she will ever be, my

garnet the truth that we were girls
    together, peering into jewelry shop
windows, plotting our beauties. Twisting
    the base of third fingers

finding want there. What did she slip
    in a pocket that day or ease
next to a breast pretending to adjust
    a strap when the male clerk
      glanced away?

Lost Twin

A block from the hospital, I see him
on the street: the other twin. No
mistaking. Once you see
a young man die, the shape of that blood
stains you. I knew
he had a brother although this other half
was absent near the end. Guilty desire
to thrive. Who would not choose
his own half-life? Recently

a woman told me many people never know
they were twinned
in the womb although born
alone. These are haunted from time to time
with feelings of loss or burdened with the sense
of needing to account
for more than one life. There are grief

groups for might-be-twins, hypnosis reaching
back to the first trimester. Mediums
who speak to lost fetuses of self
re-claiming forfeited wisdom.

Nurse, gathering the placenta, dismissed
the shrimp-perfect form of another incarnation
blaming the vision
on graveyard shift. A block away, I

see him on the sidewalk: the short, dark
athlete's hair. The hopeful shrug
of one confident shoulder. I want to call out that I
know him but I don't stop
him or know him any more than I can
halt or be-friend death. Any more than I can
know my identical
sister who swam with me one summer
when we were thumb-nail young.

Mermaid Finds Herself Upstream

She breaststrokes up river with every
muscle, eager to wash the burn
from her skin, to feel a new cold, biting not
bitter. She elbows pink fish leaping
with the same defiant will. Never

has she felt such purpose. The current
spills its mind toward an ocean
she has just shed, while she
dives pebble-bottom to forget. Storms
forced her here but navigation

is now old myth into new, an intuitive
mapping. Bird sound beckons
beyond a gull. A herd of thirsty
fur raises gentle heads in welcome.

She sucks a fresh stone, mouth full
of smooth mystery. Can one wish swim
the height of a mountain? It begins

to hail. She ells a bend, confronts
boulder-torn rapids, each fresh spray
slapping her back, back toward the familiar deep
where only moonlight matters.

Surrogate Daughter
—for AC

Who comes at the end? The long
dead? Straw bones of light? I would never
have known that hers was also my
name if not for accidental papers. She
must have been eldest, appointed proxy
during the first scare, the other cancer. This
time, after documents were snatched away,
the son presented his signature, hers replaced
for an unnamed offense.

Hospice RN, for months I visited
twice or three times a week with remedies
for everything breathless, bonded with family
the way death often introduces. Wife
with broth for one more spoon. The other
daughter with her loud brood. Son working
puzzles with pieces missing. The patient

was always glad to see me, Joanne-the-
Nurse, re-assurance of blood-pressure
and pulse. New Year stalked
his mounting hours of sleep. Liquid dribbled
from between chapped lips. No swallow.

I knelt by his bed, spoke my name
the way I always did—hearing the last sense
to abandon—and he sat up, embraced me,
weeping. *See how he loves her*, the astonished
relatives marveled. *She took away
his pain.* But I knew gratitude had no part
in this affection. He had christened her
himself and she returned in a word,
his first and final daughter.

Survivor

—for Ali

When death comes young it grows
alongside you. Shadow a little longer
than your frame. Sideways glance more curious
than compassionate. A strange, cruel
envy. You search

forbidden closets like pockets of a church
for receipt or sacrament to make
you seamless. Voice among skirts
no longer hers. In the Seer's hand

the ordinary deck grows restless. What falls out
is the Ace of Spades, the black spear
of an upside-down heart. They say she had
a heart-shaped face. I knew a man

at ninety-nine who claimed the soul doesn't end
until it has tried to become
every other life. Definition of one-hundred.
But who believes? You

need to knock down with your bare fist
all the persons and institutions and traditions
and icons who think they know
power. You want for one hot moment to be nothing
less than assassin

until you turn the gun around. People
stop you on the street to say how many pieces
of you resemble your mother: her nose, her
gesture. Martyrs are yesterdays

when we were brave. Pick up this ragged life
it is impossible to outgrow. Paint it
the color of her hair.

Part II

Lachesis the Fate Measures Tomorrow

Every gown I design is really a shroud. I
know it. The mannequins know it. Rooms
of naked facsimiles. Each garment draped
and pinned, shifted as the figure shows
its age. I have pockets of flexible

tapes, a turn-table for hemming. Patterns
tissue thin. I was born for this work: girl
in love with silk and more curious about
the body than any book or star. Task
of time and waist size. My marquee reads:
"Lachesis the Fate: Clothing for Tomorrow."

Outside my studio thousands rally,
their slogan: "Immortality for All!"
The new 'right' beyond
        housing,
            education,
                free health care
beyond what passes for war, the current
inhumanity. The next border: agelessness
which was never mine to measure.

The mannequins have gathered at the windows,
blank faces shouting back, "Be careful
what you wish for!" I set skirt lengths for next
season as one form teeters, cants, collapses.

There's always a moment when cloth fits
forever, perfect in its cut, its darts, thread woven
so skillfully few notice when it unravels.
Flesh reaching its seams. Skin understanding,
demanding earth again.

Hotel ZZZ

When the night clerk lays his head
on the counter for a minute that becomes
thirty and the last trucker has pulled
in and the first one out
is an hour from his wake-up call,

a cacophony of sigh and snore rolls under
locked doors and down hallways, up and
down stairs until the whole hotel sleeps
for once in unison. Sheets wrinkle like
suspicious eyelids welded tight. Dreams
sneak from sleep to sleep

as the guilt in 204 embraces the
anger of the couple in 336
who fought about money and then
made the best love in a decade.

And the sorrow of 127 encounters the
cowardice of 119 near the ice machine
until all the cubes melt and reform
into an ice sculpture of a
busy man taking time for his mother,
while the overweight virgin in 322 and the
jilted groom in 214 unite in erotic
fantasies both thin and forever.

The infant who curls between his
parents in 108 has no dreams
yet, but the seeds of his dreams
bury themselves in the purgatory
of the man in 333 who spent six years
in prison for the hit and run death
of a child.

Nightmares collide in the air
vents, make peace and migrate
to the 'No Vacancy' sign
where for one minute everyone
on three floors in the 40-year-old
run-down warren of borrowed beds,
whether joyous or despairing,
dreams the same delirious, desperate,
sacred hope of waking.

Blind Love

After the divorce of this or that
cousin. When rings returned or rumors
cheated, someone in the family would offer up
the great uncle from Milwaukee who married
the telephone operator. He
was blind. She had a wine-colored birth
stain emblazoned over half
her face. This was back when telephones

had voice, hers famous for its intimate
inflections. That husky whisper hooked up folks
all over the Midwest and beyond. Even
the worst news was kinder for her couplings.
Copper true and warm. Men

fantasized about what it would be
like to make love blind not just in the
dark. How every hypersensitive
member would find its home in her
curves. Women imagined

being touched hungrily, reverently, skin
savored beyond any blemish. Yes.
Yes. Yes. Those wires swung between
poles for over fifty years. No one was sure
when or if they died. But all agreed
that every necessary message raced
through every available fibre. That no ice
storm or war ever stopped her
lips, his visionary fingers.

The Nine of Cups

She called it The Wish Card, my psychic
        grandmother hoping over and over for
love although she worried most
            about money. She

took potions for sleep, a mind
        that would not settle. Ghosts
plagued her daily, hiding the coveted
        card with its brimming

chalices. Symbol of more
        than plenty. She told in alleys
and back bedrooms, for whatever
            they could give her: flour,

ribbons, plums, a bone-colored
        button. Hungry women, women
whose husbands kept the money
            as tight as an angry fist

whose only hope was fortune and greatest
        risk was wish, that many-hearted
card, the one, once found, she slipped
            under her pillow

the one her husband tore in half. Tape
        too dear, she sewed it together
like a wound. The one card now
            her fingers always found in the deck.

All the Horses Are Dying

—For Karen

You are asleep in the chair
breathing slowly through your mouth
as though tasting
the last of this world. I enter
with my stethoscope.
Crackles in your chest persist
like a hand grasping silk.

You wake slowly, pale lashes quivering,
eyes moving under lids
abandoning an anxious dream.
You tell me all the horses are dying:
the dapple, the chestnut, the one you named
Cinnamon. I offer reality's
hand, gesture of comfort, but you
persist: they are buried in the pasture now,
behind the house.
The ground there bunches in a permanent canter
of grass and clover.

What is a horse who cannot stand?
What is a horse who cannot graze?
you ask me through your grief.

I hand you twin white pills,
then a paper cup.
Even water is difficult.

You describe how you held his muzzle
in your lap, the one called Cinnamon,
counting grey hairs on his reddish chin,
both of you lying in the straw,
the sweet, pale straw
from the field where you used to gallop.

Past Life

I wear white linen, a long habit. Have forgotten the color
of my hair. Through years of prayer, the old, worn
litanies, I have earned the silence that is God. Which embraces
and invites me beyond my beautiful nothingness. Against this,
voice is less than a death wish. My brother

was the writer. He wore a crown
of thorns. With splintered hands, pressed it deeper and
deeper into his aching mind. Piercing what he knew
of lack. I never saw him happy while I

had boundless joy. I became Mother
Superior, queen of Poverty and Chastity, shaving the vanities
of young women. Hoarding, in secret, snippets
of sheen and curl. Yes, I had my sins, one
in particular. I never touched her with my

fingers. Never touched myself with her in mind. Yet our
veiled glances engendered more wishful children, more
miscarriages and abortions than any adultery. Monthly
bleeding synchronized, womanhood

no vow of Obedience could wash away. We pressed
messages into petals, tasted them in strawberry and
plum, vital as the yeast in convent
bread. We could read each other's throats, the unspent
tears, the swallow. And when I lay dying in my small, bare

cell, even then her hands held fast, bound together
in her lap. In those last moments when God demanded all
my breath, she bared her breasts to me where she had engraved
every word we never whispered, scars so perfect the blood
still wept. Then she kissed me and voice was born.

Respiration

I tell the wife and daughter, a day or two
at most, stethoscope leaving circles on moist
skin, listening, searching for one crisp breath
in a ghost town of wind. It's not

what gets in—it's what can't get out that
kills us. I remember a patient in my early
nursing days whose well-intentioned family
turned the oxygen up and up
and the young man died. The furious doctor
seething: *Carbon dioxide tells us when*
to breathe. Too much oxygen masks this need
until acid eats us alive.

Rainbows are burning the edge of atmosphere.
Mountains disappear a mere fifty miles
away, eroded by addictions
we can't even identify. Worlds intertwine

in the microcosm of a sick-room
where silk flowers from a childhood friend
offer false pollen, the real stuff poison
for lungs of no more summer. So little

comfort: a fan near closed windows, morphine,
an illogical prayer that somehow the planet's
mind recognizes the individual body
and earthquake, volcano, tsunami
will bow to a tendril of green.

The Weather Letters

The day after her passing, we found
    them like yesterday's rain: in
drawers and piled on shelves,
    stuck between magazine pages and in among
        bills: those with postmarks and the ones
she never answered.

All from a single friend, faithful to the day,
as anonymous as memory is named.

Today in the breeze we smelled sweet peas
    from the porch
Out planting hillocks of squash. Saw clouds in a
    line like white boxcars
Dust devils in the fallow field. Reminded me of the old
    dog chasing his flea-bitten tail

She slept that way, with a page curled
    in her lap, pen fallen
        to the floor.

How she used to tell us the wind never
    lies although it changes its mind
how only weather matters when years walk
        backwards with no address.

Last night we had one of those orange harvest
    sunsets. Canned 20 quarts of peaches
No rain yet but I see gray streaks over southern
    hills. It must be pouring in Centerville
Today in my slippers as I walked to the mailbox
    first frost crackled my footsteps.

Wound and Stone

They threw hard, always that envy
    between them, everything a
competition between close-born sisters.
        Others looked on.
They were hot as noon about some
    boy, picking up rocks, aiming for
a canted fencepost at the edge
        of an empty meadow.

Cheers with each hit. Another scar
    notched in gray wood, singeing
shadows. Determined to win,
        the younger sister chose a fresh missile
sharp and heavy.

Unbalanced, she missed, weight
    arcing wide flattening tall
grasses, flushing a flock of starling.
    In the wake of that dark wind, one
remained, a fledgling, left leg mangled,
        useless as lost forgiveness.

Onlookers faded into the dust of that
    day. She kept vigil, watched
as it struggled to stand, fell and fell
        again, beak opening
and closing in a silent plea for breath
    that she rhythmed in her own chest
        lacking the courage for touch.

By evening, sins lay still too deep
    to bury, next to the wounding stone.
Fragments and feather burned
    into August's drought, shrunk
under the golden shadow of geese
        into snow's anonymity.
No footsteps crossed that field,
    though her fingers often tingled
        with the soft itch for flight.

Last Straw

Scarecrow didn't winter
well. One last stalk whispers
up his left sleeve. The ragged

plaid shirt hangs on him
like sickness. His burlap
face watches field dust
more than sky. It's time

to re-seed. Clouds know it
and the crows know it. Time
to fill these furrows
with new green. The scarecrow's
hunger is for purpose
more than grain. Spring

is difficult for old men, old
women. Today or tomorrow
the field hand will hoist him
from these acres to make way

for the plow. He will lie
in his heap of broom stick bones
until someone decides
which bits are worth cobbling

into next summer's sentinel.
Young wind sifts chaff from a torn
cuff. Even broken,
his shoulders feel the grip
of tiny sparrows.

The Sunset Gene

Scientists have identified the gene
    that makes certain people weep
        when they see evening skies
turn magenta, vermillion or even
        pink. These persons reverence

any shade of sky but are transported
    by the edge of night as it bleeds
and blooms ethereal chemicals
        in designs of perfect flesh.

Men and women with this marker also
    buy roses for no reason, keep them
long after others would have thought them
        wilted. Music

inhabits their gestures. They sway even
    as they stand transfixed by
moonrise. How could a lab-man
        comprehend such DNA? Why
would researchers spend millions in

grant money to isolate crimson-clouded
    eyes? And how, in an evolutionary
sense, did sky-scape weepers even
        survive? Unless predators back then
also loved sunsets.

News People

Skin made of newspaper: black on
    white with patches of war, murder,
weather and empty crossword
      boxes. They stand

face forward with legs spread, verbs
    for eyes, seeing the
doing, and curved dark
      tears. The Daily.

But oh to be the Sunday Comics.

Bent at the waist, they ride the northbound
    bus, left by a child tired from a day,
a long journey of unwanted travel.

A grandmother who always carries
    scissors in her purse to snip out
clothing tags or carve a person.

A man in the next seat who reads
    without seeing then gladly
hands the world over
      to be re-shaped into

pirates and movie starlets or a family
    with too many mothers.

And even in the dark garage
    where they are swept
and crumpled, they still
    shout from bins in rain

or, burning, whisper partial
    names of those
convicted, those set free.

The Goodbye Skin

She asks to lie beside him for an
hour, just an hour, before earth claims him
and the smoky wind. I see her
climb onto the bed that for weeks
had housed nerve endings so brittle
the air seemed to bleed. *No*
he had screamed when she reached out

to touch him. Today his stillness is accepting
as she curls against stiff limbs. I leave
the room, closing the door softly, taping up
a makeshift sign so that no worker
on a pleasureless schedule interrupts a passion
beyond intimacy or tear. Is it possible

to reach the dead? Minutes or years later? To
beg the breeze for a fingertip or sun for the burn
of cheek against cheek? Is this what heaven
becomes: loving once again a skin
not our own? I do not see

her leave, but by the end of the shift
the room is empty, ragged cocoon. On the naked
mattress only indentations remain: head,
shoulders, buttocks, heels and next to this:
curve of a hip bone.

Thoroughbred

After the second death. After
midnights at midday and temptation
of liquor and pills, it was hooves
that saved her. After
invitations ignored, prayers torn
and burned, it took chance
to turn her around. A day
at the Races that she suspected
would be pathetic and
dull. Bus with twenty other

widows, overweight weepers throwing
their pensions away. But this was more
than ill-luck disguised as silk
and thunder, the terrible need
to run. Instantly she fell

in love with the liquid rolling animal
eyes, the nervous prancing. How a haunch
remembers not the beautiful
little man with sure hands and
a smart whip but the pure
knowledge of what each sinew
should do. A bugle. A parade. Tote
window where two dollars could buy
the ride of the lifetime. And at the

bell: wings. Yes, real wings distilled into
four legs and a neck, striking dust
from thunder, turning for
home, bunched down the Stretch. That
yearning, naked as raw
silk, to be first, to beat back blues
and yellows, every bruise, and just release
into the terrible need to live.

Planet of the Hired Men

Two widows at sundown, we spend Sunday
in the clover. On the field hill overlooking
the yellow frame farmhouse and one discouraged barn,
we ease back,
our oversized hips shifting our comfort
in double green hollows.

"If you could live anywhere," I begin the old game,
noticing in an eyelash the first evening star
like a signal to dream,
"where would it be?" expecting her to say,
"Stay here," like always
while I go to Hollywood or Maui.

"To the Planet of the Hired Men," she responds
out of the blue, still gazing overhead,
and continues: "We'd be glad we were widows
and we could watch and watch
while they bale the hay.
Their sweat would be the color of fireweed honey."
She pauses, then goes on:
"At suppertime we'd bring them wildberry pie."

"Could we eat some too?" I was wanting to know.
"Eat it and eat it," she replies, her eyes unfocussed,
clouds, pinker now, drifting over her lens.

"Just us and hired men?" I ask, still puzzling.
She nods, "And not a one over thirty."

Escalators

Esther the Mystic saw the threat
    behind everything. She told fortunes
with ordinary playing cards, futures black
      with spades spelling sickness,
ruined finances, divorces, disappointments.
  I inherited all my phobias from this
umber woman, my grandmother,
      who saw shadows
          more vividly than flesh.

She never learned to drive, traffic portending
    the ultimate disaster, but once a month
      she took the bus downtown.

Once, after a such a journey, she came home
    to describe how she saw a little girl
      get her foot caught in an escalator,
how the huge cascade of silver stairs kept moving,
    crushing down while the child screamed.

Details seeped like blood through my nine year old
    mind: the white Ked gone completely,
      shaft of bone splintered, and the terrible
        grinding pain.

How she would never dance or ride a bike, play
    hopscotch or kick ball. Never ice skate
or wear high heels, never leave me, this child
      my grandmother pasted over my eyes
so that I never take an escalator unless I
    have to and then I keep my feet
at the outermost edge, hearing that soft sobbing
      as one stair disappears into another,
        indifferent as a deck of cards.

The Cursive "I"

Graphologist, she works with the FBI
and the local police, can coax
a signature of soul
from a single letter.

The suspect sits in a metal chair
across an anonymous table. On notebook
paper, he copies the standard text.

She watches as the skyline appears
upside down: an imaginary city
complete with towers, hovels, palaces
and jails. A bare branch quivers next to
an occasional speck of flight.

As the capital "I" rises and descends,
she peers through its oval window
down a long telescope of
autumn trees toward where

a boy bends over a wooden desk. Fist
around a pencil, he strains to bend
his mind into his hand. His fingers
ache, the sarcasm of the master
wrapping them tighter and tighter
around lead, erasing him.

Until now. Under the quiet scrutiny
of this woman more mother than
interrogator, he confesses every
crime, committed or envisioned,
risking everything
to be legible again.

Séance for the Vanishing

Five at midnight, women around a talking
table. Circle on pedestal, a phantom
ballerina. They poise, fingers arching,
and summon energies.
Rock wood. Knock. One to deny. Two for affirmation.
Counting out the alphabet, one to twenty-six.

One begins: What became of a cousin,
in her mid-fifties, who went missing two summers ago
hiking in the mountains? Map-savvy. Trail-tutored.
In league with huckleberry?

A sister reveals: Over 40 people vanish in the wilderness
each year. Not one boot-print. Never even a glove.
They chant her name that ricochets and ricochets.

Table rocks twice. Last thing these branches touched
was the ankle of a woman.

The next one speaks: I see a white crow in a line
of ebony. Neither dove nor gull. Its voice is harsh. It loves
shine. Carries a bracelet in its beak, engraved, the most glittering
thing. Who will wear it now no longer warm?

Another continues: A mother is crying. When is a daughter
no longer a daughter? What makes a body disappear? Who will
shroud it now? Is there a time when girls don't lie
to their mothers?

The table warms. Spells out 'char,' the sound striking.

A fifth describes: When she was a child, she set the house on fire.
One of six, ignored, she breathed into her hands. Blew on a match,
holding it like a living tongue until it singed. Blazed the boards down.
They lived what they built and nothing was left. Scars on the
baby. The naked winters.

The table is crying, hinges keening. They rock with it,
ship at the core of storm. The white eye
of forgiveness. They hold hands now, table untouched,
moving in its own rhythm the way evergreens breathe
stealing smoke that once was woman.

Fortune Teller Advertises Free Will

It's amazing how much people pay
to hear about themselves. To know how much
it costs to love them. Or what they owe
no one. The Life Line eventually
curves around Venus. What if each of us

could choose our death, both time
and manner: I'll live as long
as I am useful. I'll live as long as I am
lovely. I'll live until
I can't bear the pain or the drugs
that exchange agony for discomfort.
I'll live until I can't remember
I am living. Then

I'll walk across seawater, pelicans
rising and plunging alongside me. I'll
hold my breath as my ankles
go under. I'll dissolve
like stirred ash. I'll taste the salt
I always crave. I will join the many
who moon-breathe. Someday I'll

take the drug that gives me
one more dream: Birthdays. A favorite
city to pace alone. Coupling, crying
out at the end which is always
endless. One man dreamed
of giving a speech while the whole world
listened. He could
remember the words but not repeat
them because he too
was listening. Which is why
the Fortune Teller advertises Free
Will. And why she costs a fortune.

Part III

Atropos the Fate Dismantles Her Own Altar

Replicas of my shears rust in museums. Thieves out-think
code to touch the blood of those blades. As though memory
of war could make them brave. As though legend explains—
bad luck to say it—death. In case

your myths are sketchy, I'm the Fate that snips, the ultimate
Fortune. Tarot card with an edge bent down. I watch

another launch, private sector invading Space with a ship labeled
Youth Unlimited. Better to re-seed the mountaintop. Better
to sign on for the invisible circus of the brain. My metal

is as illusory as the vision that hangs in the sky for a silver
tremor after the blast. When the pilot has two beats
to bank away. No one hand could sabotage so many breaths

in a nano-second. A city's arteries under a mega-flower becoming
flame, the confounder of paper and scissors. Don't you realize
I took my own life eons ago? Fascinated by my power
but needing practice? Scientist injecting herself with disease
so sure of her miracle cure. All Fate

is collective. The end disproved by one selfless citizen
or cell. Ghosts are a comforting legend: sisters in an attic
mixing thread with destiny. Come, Children,

look at guns under glass. At Oppenheimer and the Curies.
Then tell me if you believe in an old woman with a jackknife
in her pocket. Each of you fingering the trigger up your sleeve.

Radio Bath

Music bubbles around your pale
body, white but not
the blue-white of death. Stubbornly
your eyes stay sheathed
wanting me to believe the terrible
act you staged. I

am nineteen. You are disappointed
that I am not my mother. That I reserve
despair only for the young. I unplug
the cord and water pours from
the black box I lift from your
cold bath. Grandmother,

I grieve my lack
of patience, that I couldn't see
the torment, worn as a deck
of cards, all your thumbprints. You begin
to shudder and weep. I am repulsed
by the bloat of your nakedness, the gray dust
at your crotch. I toss a towel,
turn away.

II

You seduced him with death again
and again, your blank-faced
husband whose hands loved
field work. You hated
that he beat you to it: the slick
rain of November's curve.

III

Your older sister Ruth
met gypsies first, gathered in alleys
behind the rented house.
They laid cards on burlap
around the burning drum, an oily
warmth. Women, disguised,

exchanged pennies for any
future. You lived between superstitions
and envy. Ruth met fortune
first, but you the better Seer,
thrust hands into fire, revealing over
and over what no one
wanted to know.

IV

I was nineteen the day I learned
Palmistry. I stole the only knowledge
you never earned: Tarot, Astrology, Ouija,
Séance but never
flesh. I knew to trace the life line
last.

V.

The radio is ruined. No way now
to listen for stars. Some nights I go back,
kneel beside cold porcelain,
trail my hand in still
water. You had read that if electricity
meets water the heartbeat
can't survive. I know better.
How nerves run on risk,
clairvoyant.

In the Millinery Shop
—For Esther

I enter, ringing tiny bells.
Three sisters lean over a work
bench of feathers, bows,
and blossoms in the shop
that was their living. They do
and don't expect me, lean closer
over patterns, protecting
secret style.

I cannot turn my back any more than
I can wake. My hands are ivory,
my clothes in sepia, the stain
of old photos laid out in autumn light.

Ruth coughs and adds a daisy. She
outlived tuberculosis to die instead
in childbirth at the end of her 29th year.
Marguerite smiles, re-arranges blonde curls.

"Grandmother," I whisper to the middle
one, who is art, who lived out the terror
of her older sister's death and in envy
of how her younger sister mastered
every avenue of love. She traces

the faceless mannequin filling in
brows. Under cover of these rooms
she captures futures, flirts with ecstasy and black
veiled despair. Imagines the someday
of my mother. Tonight I

measure, snip and hand her satin
ribbon that she winds carefully through
straw, inspects, satisfied, shaping my helix
from the distance of a dream.

The New CPR

We no longer breathe for each other. No
longer need that anonymous lip lock that for years
spelled salvation. Strangers walked away
from possible mouth-to-mouth
contagion and besides, scientists say,
there is enough oxygen stored in the bloodstream
to keep flesh alive if we just

compress. A hundred beats a minute. Like
struggling uphill toward a cathedral
of need, jogging home for supper or
sprinting down some spring-soaked
avenue to propose to courage. Whatever knocking
it takes to get this stopped muscle
to repeat itself.

I find that space two fingers up from the
sternum. Ball one fist and cap it
with my other hand. The 911 operator
counts for me. I whistle toward
the moon, take in clouds still ripe
with sunset. All the while listening

beyond earshot for sirens announcing
trained hands and a defibrillator. And after,
when they have revived the body—or not—
am I allowed a kiss then? Or am I
forever denied the electricity of skin? True
cardiac flint?

Old Growth

Hospital, the highest point in town. From a top floor
    window, nurse of thirty years sees past
fog, farther than the ebbing eternity of trees. She
    has bandaged every limb.

Each midnight she hears stories
    of doctors' civilized wives, who,
in spite of wealth, status, even love, left
    this coast where chainsaw
is king and suicide

his queen. Seas too cold to swim yield
    perfect fish at the price of breath. So many
drownings; so seldom a body. No man
    ever wins here. No woman marries

well, counting rings: a hundred, two hundred,
    three. Bad roads tremble with logging
trucks' overload. Night nurse sighs
    as an ambulance winds up the switchback
trail, red and screaming: a broken

chain, misplaced fall, the spike, hidden. Under
    cedar, fir, and hemlock nightshift
    never ends.

The Breath Mirror

They say that on calm nights after a death
you can hear the clop-clop of the old physician's
horse, creak of buggy wheels, traveling
back roads. Hoof prints and grooves
guide the sway-backed pony
homeward, doctor's body nodding, slack
with weariness. Maybe the crossing

was better then. No pulsing lights blinding
the dilated pupil or screen tracking mountains
no real heart traveled. No machine
forcing oxygen where lavender and
leavened bread suffice. Curtains move wind

into midnight. A cool rag is turned,
rinsed, rung, and turned again. Sighs
sift forgiveness. From the hallway,
hinge and a candle. Opiate seeps
bitter between flaking lips as the chest

stills. Then he who has sworn to first
do no harm, slips a flat plate of silver
where no mist condenses. Calls this
his breath mirror though made
for beauty. Heads home wiping souls
from its face.

Hired Horses at Seaside

Their manes rise, strand upon strand,
with bleached grasses in wind from the surf.
Tethered between dunes: beach horses for rent.
Bondage as regular as tides;
down sand and back, down sand and back.

Summer and winter on the west coast they wait,
sand-dappled, rumps to the wind,
cropping bitter fodder. Salt spray makes them blind
in less than a year, old in sea time.

They do not wish or weep. Know only
patience by the backbone: quarter mile down the beach
and back, hooves cracking sand dollars and clam shells,
voices keen as gulls'
if they could speak
or rise on hidden wings.

It is late morning when the first children mount,
believing in withers as wild as the sea,
flinging themselves on Pegasus' neck:
down and back, down and back,
leaving a trail of half-moons.

So that when at last the ponies sleep
in their shed near the rumble of night-tides,
white eyes open,
they form someone else's dream,
a kind of white nightmare:
moon-rumor of what the sea can do.

Teaching the Wound

Assume pain, I tell them, the young, the
minimum-waged, those who work the midnight
shift with no chance for stars. We lean
over the bed of a 93-year-old man with advanced
Parkinson's Disease. His face is
frozen, even his eyes don't seem to move
unless you watch the sheen. These

Student Aides are to turn him, bathe and lotion
his stiffened limbs. After they roll him silent
and awkward as a rug, I notice the bandage
discolored with seepage, covering his left
calf. The notes had not mentioned

a wound. Someone should have given
him a pill, an elixir, some remedy before we started
the fumbling torture of water and
rag. I ring for the med nurse, emphasizing
again: *Can you understand that most patients*

in this situation would be feeling pain? One
is texting when he thinks I don't
see. Another turns her head fingering her
hair in the mirror over the tiny sink. Another
glances at the clock. Two whisper together.
I can teach skills and charting aimed at avoiding
termination and litigation, how to keep a

license clean, but it is next to impossible to force
someone to leave their own
body, crawl beneath flesh still warm beyond
sense or usefulness. True pain is
individual. I turn back to the bed. The girl
with the basin of water that she has
checked three times for temperature without

being told, the one with almost no
English, rinses the cloth and parts
skin folds, all the time murmuring
into his silence, reassuring him, speaking
his name that even I had forgotten.

Into the Mirror

The reflected room is not quite
equal: vase with a different cut
of crystal. Door further
ajar. Draped chemise holds scents
of another woman's body.

Time-of-day seems similar: shadows
of just-past-afternoon. Flowers
in the reflection just an hour
older. The uncapped lipstick speaks
a forgotten dialect. Can vanity

explain silver discrepancies? Does
one blemish shift life, make it
truer to the double sense? And if

no eyes stare into the room-within-a-
room, who would ever notice this subtle
dissymmetry? She presses her palm
against its opposite until fingers
coalesce. A bracelet

follows, then a profile, a mind, the rich
brown of her newly tinted
hair. Both rooms become pond-still.
The finest pane separates an off-hand
glance from the moment
a woman realizes she has aged
and chooses, then,
to disappear.

Sacred Shadows

—for Patrick

We were ten the summer you told me
you believed in God. I remember
clover interwoven in green lawn and how
we could smell the ocean although it was
miles away. I confessed that I

believed in him too, had seen him, in fact,
in the hallway outside my bedroom
the night my father died, the two
of them watching as only shadows do. You
still wore your polio leg braces

which is why we sat in evergreen
shade discussing theology while other
children climbed monkey bars. We agreed
on the divine of dim places, flash
striking pine branches overhead. You
confided you had seen him too in the hospital
room the night your roommate

passed. Silence rising from the bed
of a six-year-old boy like icy smoke of an
evaporating rainbow, drifting
your way. You knew then you could join
him in this soft reprieve, little soul
you had shared so many agonies with and also
jokes and guessing games. But nurses

arrived and drew the curtains. This world
within a world within a world holds
the greatest shine. All the high butterflies
were ours. How I loved you at that moment,
mistaking death for God. I have no idea

where you are all these years later. If you became
a priest like you pledged that July afternoon. I
became a nurse but not
a nun. Have seen them many times since,
those two interchangeable friends
walking in the dark, arm in arm.

Tiny House of Sons

A good ten feet above my stepladder, a bird
house swings, anchored to hemlock,
adopted as its own. Camouflage
of moss and upward growth almost
erase it. A neighbor

told me the three sons of a long-ago tenant
built it, quarreling over nails
and glue. Six hands on a hammer, then sawing.
Stones hold a book open, door drilled
the diameter of wrens. Those boys

have grown now into gossip: the oldest
in business with his father, middle one
in prison. Something second-degree. The youngest
meditative, lost in Asia or the Andes. I rake

maple and alder leaves, see the tiny house
more clearly now, door blocked by twig
and down. Rocking like a childhood
floor where all marbles roll. They

jostled each other on the ladder, fighting
to be the one to twist wire over
a limb. Wood into woodlands. I still
find nails among huckleberry. Under cedar
a rusty tape measure. Which one

watched from a window: plain brown
bird with grasses in her beak? Which one
collected June's fragment of shell?
And who, at a desk, in a cell, lost in
forests, still practices that whistle?

Eyes Like Trunk or Wingtip

It wasn't weather. It wasn't
the crumple of metal against
metal that stifled traffic that
Monday a.m. Frustration drumming
the wheel. Music talk skipping
station to station. It was a
wound. As I crept

forward peering through rain arcs, I
saw the squirrel inching its way across
four lanes, front muscles dragging
its crushed back legs. Around me
the blurry framed worry of other faces
dissolved from time to
empathy. I wished for a
morphine syringe

but came up with only a remembered
conversation about how elephants grieve
and also geese, circling their
dead, heads lowered, touching
with trunk or wing. How naïve
to be amazed as though dying
was a secret. Now

it is my turn to pass. I take with
me how a downed leaf clings to gray
fur, how eyes focus only
on impossible banks, winter and
hunger fading. Smear of blood
on the road like holy oil

as travelers brake, avoid a further
hit, inch congealed into slow swerves
that make us not more human
but purely animal.

Unbraided

I comb my hair after hiking
    all day in the woodlands. I grip
the brush with its stiff bristles
    and wooden handle

and stroke and stroke. A shine
    comes up, glimmer of river water
washed from a gray sky. Knot
    like a branch, reaching. Webs

cling white, the thinnest humming
    strings. Scent of pitch and needles
lingers from where I paused
    to catch my breath.

Trace of smallest lives nests in me
    tonight. Vein from a leaf. Thread
of a feather. Mushroom gill and spores
    of moss worshipping

the fixed star. These I pull from my
    hair with the skill of breezes. What my
eyes could not take in by day
    my evening brush remembers.

The Weatherman's Widow

Two mounds under a snowfield. Washed out
bridge. Pressure of wind-shift, star-plots,
sun-tantrum. Corn stalks crooked
in a hungry field demonized
him. Yet in times of plenty

he was savior. When tornados turned
he was a god. And so it is
after his passing. And I have become
the keeper of his shrine: weathervane
thin and buffeted.

I married the storm in him. Midnights
of the empty bed when he paced attic rafters
carving up the moon. Charts weighted
with igneous. Barometer like a slow, insane clock.

Casseroles appear on my doorstep with prayers
for fair weddings. Coin in a hand-
stitched sac, faux-seed for fruitful
fields. Babies named for his sunrise, mine
now. We had no children

but his rough, dawn-light predictions. I dip
my brush into its color. Wash a strip beyond
black mountains. Wait for it to dry
before I hang it on tomorrow. Another cabbage
bribes my doorstep. Only the unknown
is holy.

Fire Mare

I have driven this road twice a week
    since September, passing this field
first on my left, then to my right,
        returning. I have glanced with half
a mind at the acre of fading grasses,
    noticed the vague shape of a horse, grazing.

This terrain is like much of any life:
    a tangent, perimeter of thought, not wholly
present, not my field.

Today, as I turn, heading east around the
    curve, I am shocked into vision. The rain
has stopped and a slow sun has chosen
        this ordinary scene. A sorrel mare stands
by the fence in halo, each hair of her
    coppery coat illuminated, a precise shining,
        an equine star.

I cannot look away. She owns this moment
    as though I have never seen a horse before,
never acknowledged what the torched grace of winter
    can do to the soul.

But there are cars behind me and my next
    patient waits. I drive on, straining in the
rear view mirror for one more glimpse of brilliance,

see only silhouette: dark horse, an empty
    shape of what we hope to know.

Black-and-Womb

Hers is the last picture in a long-ago album
about war. Black-and-white
courtship. She faces directly into
the blind snapping Brownie's eye. Her lips
don't move but she tells us
she is pregnant. Maybe it's the smock,
hem uneven, futile billow over a thin, young
body left behind. Who shuttered

this image? My grandmother? The maid-of-
honor herself dating a sailor? Jilted
suitor forgotten in a dance-step? It's natural
to question what might-have-been. Sister,
what did you do to my future five years
in the distance?

Behind her gardens wilt after a quick
wedding. It was hot that summer
in shipped-out army-green. Alone in shops
the new bride flashed her glass
diamond, fingers of gossip counting off
months. Her hands will never change

the pain of that baby. And night cries haven't
reached the mourners over-seas. Sister,
no matter how many trunks I
dust, no flash ever captured blue
or brown eyes. Go back to sleep in the vast
Pacific under her lungs. This picture
your only likeness.

Voice Print

It's no longer fingertips that acquit or
solve. News: Speech Imprints. Recognition. Lips
and throat in league to send a thief
to prison. To secure a license to hunt
or wed. Breath shouted

in a whisper so distinctive the sound of it
makes a grown man shudder and cover
his ears. Not me. Not me.

Is speech inherited or taught? Clicking
of a rolled tongue. Fame in the whistle
of pursed lips. Social terror in the swollen larynx
of a teenaged gulp. They chose five hundred subjects.
Had them read the same anonymous sentence
without expression. *As you might read
the phone book. If you knew none*

of the names. Yet quiver lurks in every Smith
and Wyzinski. I remember an autumn mountain
where I fell in love with one rogue syrinx though I never
saw the bird. Voice is a heart-skip

away from lying. Or loss. And stutter goes on
forever. Even Shakespeare cannot mask
the actor. Rumor of my earliest word
hums between Neptune and its moons. I speak
where I wish to enter. Am convicted
by the wind.

The Stone Masons

Not out of faith, but stone. Two men,
atheists both, built the town's
church. Rock rivered
to the smoothness of loaves. Heft
and sweat. The mortar.

         This was no
cathedral. No tower for bells. No crimson
or indigo windows. In those hard times
they toiled for food alone and a place
to sleep where silence breathed
its deep calm. They seldom spoke,
yet there was always communion
between them. July sun
called the house of god upwards
though neither of them believed; the war
had been too hard.

They married
sisters. Lived in the city. And after
one of them lost his mind, the other
sat daily at the bedside, accepting,
while the women prayed. He recalled
then some remnant of Bible lore
from childhood when Christ, fasting,
was tempted by the Devil
to turn rocks into bread.
And he had refused. Let stones

be stones, indifferent to weather,
worship, what breaks a man and what
builds him.

The Daily Séance

Memory, vision or dream? I see
my mother singing in the sunset. How her hands
always found the keys after hearing
a melody once. She is teaching me
the pinks or is it vermillion?

Vision, memory or dream? I sense a child
weeping. Is she my sister
trying to breathe? Is she my unchosen
gene, future's other road, my interrupted
peace? Dream, vision

or memory? The day my father died
I fed him tea from a spoon. I feel steam
against my cheeks. Rarely polish
silver fearing my upside-down reflection
in the concave view that includes
opening lips.

Gesture of smoke in a fireless room.
One fold of curtain, moving. Questions

from those who've passed seem prosaic:
Did you feed the cat? Are my roses
blooming? Alone. Alone. I must
respond with the truth. The Tabby
ran away. Deer ate all the roses.

Memory, vision or dream? My grandfather
forgetting every name, even his own, even
the familial ones: father, brother,
grandpa. Until the day before the final one.
A small bird flew in the room. Past
the stained wallpaper and torn vinyl.

The attendant opened windows. Still, it circled
and circled. All the silent voices. Until he
spoke one thing: my mother's name
in a waking question. I meet
that word sometimes. My middle name,
long-buried lyric, in a memory, a dream, a sparrow.

Goddess of Anger and Shame

What if we are all are made from goddess'
names? Not only bones, attributes, DNA, but also
the calling? Mine is a mythos of anger
and shame: *Mokosh*, brought across an ocean
by a penniless drunk—not poet or dissident—
whose liquored fists whipped
but never worshipped ten shoeless children.

Five aunts all married young, changing surnames
in their teens. All four uncles, drafted,
wounded in the field. Their only holy memory:
how my father, the eldest son, brained the old man
with a two-by-four fracturing that altar
for good. I feel brazen, claiming

a goddess, even a flawed one unearthed
on the Internet by chance: Mokos, Moksha,
Makash. Never written. Slavs lettered late. She
is the exhaustion of a field-dream, agony
of the final stage of childbirth.
Feast day: Any Friday. Symbol: a breast-shaped
stone. I admit I search for heaviness
to lay against my chest. A metamorphic nipple.

Her few statues chisel a large head, simian
arms, mannish hands. Fingers of a weaver that translate
to Fate. I see her biting the tough wool
of a final thread with horse teeth. Thanks a lot,
Grandpa-I-Never-Met, whose liver failed, pagan,
years before my birth. Who willed me, if not Venus'
limbs, an ancient word for "moisture,"
bowlegged initial I am learning to forgive.

About the Author

Joanne M. Clarkson's previous collections include *Believing the Body*, published in 2014 by Gribble Press. She was awarded a Grant for Artist Projects from Artist Trust of Washington to help her complete *The Fates*. Her poem "Klotho the Fibre Goddess Describes Fate" won first place in Northern Colorado Writers Annual Competition in 2015 and "Survivor" was selected by Emrys Journal in 2016 for their Nancy Dew Taylor "excellence in the art of poetry" award. Joanne has loved poetry since she was a child and her work has appeared in over 200 magazines and journals internationally. She has Master's Degrees in English and Library Science, has taught and worked as a professional librarian. After caring for her mother through a long illness, she re-careered as a Registered Nurse specializing in Home Health and Hospice care. In the spring of 2016, she published her first nonfiction book: *There's Always a Miracle: True Stories of Life Before and After Death,* about her time as a Hospice RN. Joanne lives in Olympia, Washington, with her husband James. She serves on the Board of the Olympia Poetry Network.

About the Book

The Fates was designed by Bertha Rogers; the art on the cover is a mixed media work titled "Two Birds Speaking." The typeface for the cover is Adobe CS InDesign News 701 Book Type; and the typeface for the text is Adobe CS InDesign Garamond Book type. Lawrence E. Shaw proofread the text and front matter. The book was printed on 60-lb. offset, acid-free, recycled paper in the United States of America. This first edition is limited to copies in paper wrappers.

About Bright Hill Press

OUR MISSION: To seek out, study, and collect the work of early and contemporary writers, storytellers, and artists, and to publish, disseminate, and present that work through publications and educational and public programs for the larger community.

OUR HISTORY: Bright Hill Press/Word Thursdays was founded in 1992 by Bertha Rogers, with Ernest M. Fishman. A writer, teacher, and visual artist, Ms. Rogers serves as the organization's executive director and editor in chief. Mr. Fishman has served BHP as president and/or chief financial officer since its beginnings. Bright Hill Press is located at Bright Hill Literary Center, 94 Church Street, in the hamlet of Treadwell, in New York's Catskill Mountain Region; program participants are from Delaware, Otsego, Sullivan, Schoharie, Broome, and Chenango counties as well. Programs and services have grown to meet the stated and implied needs of both youth and adult populations in those counties, as well as the needs of the literary community in New York State and beyond. BHP's current administrative focus is on long-range planning, in order to better fulfill its mission and expand its programs.

OUR ARTISTIC PHILOSOPHY: Bright Hill Press is dedicated to increasing audiences' appreciation of the writing arts and oral traditions that comprise American literature, and to encouraging and furthering the tradition of oral poetry and writing in the Catskills. Writers and artists who participate in BHP's programs are selected for their artistic excellence, their ability and willingness to work within a community setting, and the diversity of their backgrounds, genres, and styles. BHP understands that recognition of the need for a literary community and a commitment to lifelong learning are critical aspects of audience development; the organization's programs for children and adults engender the spirit, craft, and imagination that make this possible.

OUR PROGRAMS are offered to people of all ages. Current program offerings include:
- Word Thursdays, a reading series begun in 1992 and presenting open readings followed by readings and discussion by featured authors;
- Bright Hill Books, publishing anthologies as well as poetry collections and chapbooks and interdisciplinary collections by individual authors since 1994;
- New York State's Literary Web Site, nyslittree.org (since 1999), and the New York State Literary Map (in print and online), developed and administered by BHP, in partnership with the New York State Council on the Arts;
- Word Thursdays Share the Words HS Poetry Mentoring Program and Competition, affording young poets a chance to write and present their own poetry in a public competition since 1996;
- Word Thursdays Literary Workshops for Kids & Adults, offering, since 1994, innovative programs that celebrate and incorporate the elegant use of words with other disciplines;
- BHLC Internship Program for College and HS Students, offering, since 1994, students an opportunity to learn the business of literature.
- Bright Hill Presents: Annual History & Nonfiction Day; Chamber music in the

library; and Songs from the Great American Songbook

OUR FACILITIES include The Bright Hill Literary Center Complex:
- BHLC Education Wing, a year-round facility for writing and visual arts classes;
- The Word & Image Gallery, dedicated, since 2002, to presenting works by regional and national artists that integrate words and images;
- Bright Hill Library & Internet Wing, since 2004, a facility with more than 15,000 titles of prose and poetry, art, reference, nature, and children's books for the immediate and larger community;
- Patterns Literary Garden & The Secret Garden, an outdoor space for the whole community, landscaped and created by Catskill Outdoor Educational Corps, a program of Americorps at SUNY Delhi;
- The Kitchen Bookstore, with used books of all genres;
- Offices for staff;
- Guest rooms for visiting and in-residency writers and artists.

GOVERNANCE: Bright Hill Press/Word Thursdays is an independent 501 (c) (3), not-for-profit corporation governed by a board of directors representing the community the organization serves, and an advisory board from the larger community.

Bright Hill Press Books

Bright Hill Press Poetry Book Award Series

The Fates
Joanne M. Clarkson   2017 $16
2016 Poetry Book Award, Chosen by Richard Foerster

Final Fort
Caroline Morrell   2016 $16
2015 Poetry Book Award, Chosen by Alice B. Fogel

The Hydromantic Histories
Fox Frazier-Foley   2015 $16
2014 Poetry Book Award, Chosen by Chard DeNiord

Tonight's Quiet
Constance Norgren   2014 $16
2013 Poetry Book Award, Chosen by Alfred Corn

What I Can Tell You
Ruth Moon Kempher   2013 $16
2012 Poetry Book Award, Chosen by Philip Mosley

Outside Come In
Ryan J. Browne   2012 $16
2010 Poetry Book Award, Chosen by Neil Shepard

Almond Town
Margaret Young   2011 $16
2009 Poetry Book Award, Chosen by Colette Inez

Raven's Paradise
Red Hawk   2010 $16
2008 Poetry Book Award, Chosen by Rhina Espaillat

Infinite Beginnings
Lucyna Prostko 2009 $16
2007 Poetry Book Award, Chosen by Joan Larkin

How the Brain Grew Back Its Own History
Liz Beasley 2008 $14
2006 Poetry Book Award, Chosen by Jay Rogoff

Need-Fire
Becky Gould Gibson   2007 $14
2005 Poetry Book Award, Chosen by Liz Rosenberg

The Artist As Alice: From a Photographer's Life
Darcy Cummings 2006 $14
2004 Poetry Book Award, Chosen by Carolyne Wright

The Aerialist
Victoria Hallerman 2005 $12
2003 Poetry Book Award. Chosen by Martin Mitchell

Strange Gravity
Lisa Rhoades 2004 $12
2002 Poetry Book Award, Chosen by Elaine Terranova

The Singer's Temple
Barbara Hurd 2003 $12
2001 Poetry Book Award, Chosen by Richard Frost

Heart, with Piano Wire
Richard Deutch 2002 $12
2000 Poetry Book Award, Chosen by Maurice Kenny

My Father & Miro & Other Poems
Claudia M. Reder 2001 $12
1999 Poetry Book Award, Chosen by Colette Inez

Traveling Through Glass
Beth Copeland Vargo 2000 $12
1998 Poetry Book Award, Chosen by Karen Swenson

To Fit Your Heart into the Body
Judith Neeld 1999 $12
1997 Poetry Book Award, Chosen by Richard Foerster

Blue Wolves
Regina O'Melveny 1997 $12
1996 Poetry Book Award, Chosen by Michael Waters

My Own Hundred Doors
Pam Bernard 1996 $10
1996 Poetry Book Award, Chosen by Carol Frost

Bright Hill Press Poetry Book Series

Good Question
Sally Fisher   2015 $16

Orenoque, Wetumka, & Other Poems
Robert Bensen   2012 $18

Flares and Fathoms
Margot Farrington 2005 $14

Every Infant's Blood
Graham Duncan 2002 $14.95

Bright Hill Press At Hand Poetry Chapbook Award Series

Passing Through Blue Earth Cynthia Neely   2016 $10
(2015 Poetry Chapbook Award)
Heirloom Bulldog Lynn McGee 2015 $10
(2014 Poetry Chapbook Award)
Language You Refuse to Learn Claudia M. Stanek 2014 $10
(2013 Poetry Chapbook Award)
The Cards We've Drawn Scot Slaby 2014 $10
(2013 Poetry Chapbook Award)
Self-Portrait/Sixteen Sevenlings   Rodger Moody   2013 $10
(2012 Poetry Chapbook Award)
A Tide of A Hundred Mountains Richard Levine   2012 $10
(2011 Poetry Chapbook Award)
Counterpoint Jean Hollander   2011 $10
(2010 Poetry Chapbook Award)
The Infatuations and Infidelities of Pronouns
Christopher Bursk   2011 $10
(2009 Poetry Chapbook Award)
Haywire Rachel Contreni Flynn 2009 $10
(2007 Poetry Chapbook Award)
The Cut Worm Douglas Korb 2008 $8
(2006 Poetry Chapbook Award)
A Sense of Place Bhikshuni Weisbrot 2007 $8
(2005 Poetry Chapbook Award)
Gobbo: A Solitaire's Opera David Cappella 2006 $8
(2004 Poetry Chapbook Award)
Web-Watching Bruce Bennett 2005 $8
(2003 Poetry Chapbook Award)
Possum Shelby Stephenson 2004 $8
(2002 Poetry Chapbook Award)
First Probe to Antarctica Barry Ballard 2003 $8
(2001 Poetry Chapbook Award)
Inspiration Point Matthew J. Spireng 2002 $8
(2000 Poetry Chapbook Award)

What Falls Away Steve Lautermilch 2001 $8
(1999 Poetry Chapbook Award)
Whatever Was Ripe William Jolliff 1999 $8
(1997 Poetry Chapbook Award)
The Man Who Went Out for Cigarettes
Adrian Blevins 1996 $8   (1995 Poetry Chapbook Award)

Bright Hill Press At Hand Fiction Chapbook Award Series

Low Country Stories Lisa Harris $8
(1996 Fiction Chapbook Award)
Boxes Lisa Harris $8
(1998 Fiction Chapbook Award)

Bright Hill Press At Hand Poetry Chapbook Series

Other People's Stories Barbara Elovic 2014 $10
Dancing Bears Karen Fabiane 2011 $10
A Plastic Bag of Red Cells Annie Petrie-Sauter 2010 $10
Skunk Night Sonnets Daniel Waters 2009 $10
The Wooden Bowl Sharon Ruetenik 2009 $10
Love in the End Mary Kay Rummel 2008 $10
Effects of Sunlight in the Fog Alan Catlin 2008 $10
Picking Up Evelyn Duncan 2008 $8
The Lily Poems Liz Rosenberg 2008 $8
The Courtship and Other Tales Kathryn Ugoretz 2007 $8
Hairpin Loop Anne Blonstein 2007 $8
The Coriolis Effect Michael Dowdy 2007 $8
It Does Not Julia Suarez 2006 $8
In Late Fields Steven Ostrowski 2006 $8
Instinct Joanna Straughn 2006 $8
Autobiography of My Hand Kurt S. Olsson 2006 $8
Degrees of Freedom Nicholas Johnson 2006 $8
Walking Back the Cat Lynn Pattison 2005 $8
The Spirit of the Walrus ElisaVietta Ritchie 2005 $8
LightsOut Tom Lavazzi 2005 $8
The Last Best Motif Naton Leslie 2005 $6

Bright Hill Press Anthologies

Speaking the Words Anthology 1994 $6.95
Edited by Bertha Rogers

The Word Thursdays Anthology of Poetry & Fiction 1995 $12.95
Edited by Bertha Rogers

The Second Word Thursdays Anthology:
Poetry & Prose by Bright Hill Press Writers 1999 $19.95
Edited by Bertha Rogers

Bright Hill Press Word & Image Series

Suddenly There Were Leaves $22
Poetry & Prose by Main View Gallery & Studio Artists
Edited by Bertha Rogers

How Looking Becomes Seeing:
Word Thursdays Youth Workshops Museum Research, Writing, & Visual Art Program
Edited by Bertha Rogers $20 (forthcoming)

Breathing the Monster Alive
Eric Gansworth 2006 $16
On the Watershed:

The Natural World of New York's Catskill Mountain Region/
Poetry & Prose by Catskill Student Writers
Edited by Bertha Rogers 2001 $14.95

Out of the Catskills & Just Beyond
Literary & Visual Works by Catskill Writers & Artists
Edited by Bertha Rogers 1997 $24

Iroquois Voices, Iroquois Visions
A Celebration of Contemporary Six Nations Arts
Edited by Bertha Rogers, with Maurice Kenny,
Tom Huff, & Robert Bensen 1996 $15

Bright Hill Press Exhibition Series

Bright Hill Book Arts 2010 $16
Edited by Bertha Rogers
Curated by Elsi Vassdal Ellis & Bertha Rogers

Bright Hill Book Arts 2008 $16
Edited by Bertha Rogers
Juried by Keith Smith & Bertha Rogers

Bright Hill Book Arts 2007 $16
Edited by Bertha Rogers
With commentary by Karen Hanmer & Bertha Rogers

Bright Hill Book Arts 2006 $16
Edited by Bertha Rogers
With commentary by Richard Minksy & Bertha Rogers

Bright Hill Book Arts 2005 $16
Edited by Bertha Rogers
With commentary by Edward Hutchins & Bertha Rogers

Bright Hill Book Arts 2004 $12
Edited by Bertha Rogers
With commentary by Nancy Callahan & Louise Neaderland

Bright Hill Book Arts 2003 $10
Edited by Bertha Rogers
With commentary by Rory Golden & Keith Smith

Bright Hill Book Arts 2002 $10
Edited by Bertha Rogers
With commentary by Richard Minsky & Peter Verheyen

Ordering Bright Hill Press Books

BOOKSTORES & INDIVIDUALS: Bright Hill Press books are distributed to the trade and to the public by Small Press Distribution (spdbooks.com), 1341 Seventh Street Berkeley, CA 94710-1409; Baker & Taylor, 44 Kirby Ave., POB 734, Somerville, NJ 08876-0734; and North Country Books (regional titles), 311 Turner St., POB 217, Utica, NY 13501-1727. Our books may also be found at BN.com, Amazon.com, at your local bookstores, and at Bright Hill Press's website, brighthillpress.org (payment may be made by credit card and/or through PayPal). If your local bookstores do not stock Bright Hill Press books, please ask them to special order, or write to us at Bright Hill Press, 94 Church Street, Treadwell, NY 13846-4607 or to our e-mail address: wordthur@stny.rr.com, or call at 607-829-5055. Further information may be found on our website: brighthillpress.org; or by calling 607-829-5055.

Bright Hill Press and Literary Center, 94 Church Street, Treadwell, NY 13846